PESSIMISMS

www.pessimisms.com

PESSIMISMS

*Famous (and not so famous) Observations, Quotations, Thoughts,
and Ruminations on What to Expect When You're Expecting the Worst*

ERIC MARCUS

CLIENT DISTRIBUTION SERVICES

NEW YORK, NY

All quotes by Ashleigh Brilliant copyright © 2003.

www.ashleighbrilliant.com

Copyright acknowledgments continue on page 160.

First Edition

ISBN 1-59315-000-8

Library of Congress Cataloging-in-Publication
data available upon request.

Cover and book design by Elliot Joel Stern.

10 9 8 7 6 5 4 3 2 1

To my

Grandma Ethel,

who always told me,

"I'll never live

to see you married."

(She was right.)

Contents

There are people, lots of them, who see a silver lining behind every dark cloud. Then there was my Grandma Ethel. For her, behind every dark cloud was another dark cloud. And a cloudless sky was no reason to celebrate. Although she was a very good-hearted and devoted grandmother, she could take a sunny day, any sunny day, and turn it into a potential tragedy: "You could die from heat stroke on such a day!" And winter? Some people picture crystalline snowflakes and bracing walks in the woods. Not Grandma. At the first sign of frost, we could always count on a phone call from Brooklyn warning us of the dangers we'd likely encounter just outside of our door: "Don't walk on frozen ponds,"

PESSIMISMS

she'd insist in her deeply accented English, "you could fall through and drown." "But Grandma," I'd explain, "where we live in Queens, there *are* no ponds."

Despite my protests, Grandma's pessimistic prognostications arrived with every conversation, sometimes backed up by printed proof. Few things seemed to please her more than to come across an article in one of the New York tabloids about the latest tragedy to snuff out the life of an unwitting child. "See?" she would say, holding out the article as proof that her worries were grounded in fact, "These things happen. So don't say I didn't warn you."

As luck would have it, Grandma Ethel passed on some of her pessimistic genes to me, although my pessimism is thankfully tempered by the optimistic genes I inherited from my Grandma May, who never let life's vicissitudes get in the way. So if Grandma Ethel's mantra was, "Expect the worst," and Grandma May's was, "Hope for the best," mine is, "Expect the worst, but hope for the best."

Despite my relatively evenhanded outlook on life, I've been sorely disappointed over the years when looking for just the right kind of inspiration at my local bookstore.

Introduction

I always hope for the best, but inevitably leave empty-handed.
And no wonder. The shelves groan under the weight of books
filled with sunny, soupy, stories. Affirmation books. Self-actual-
ization books. Daily meditation books. Happy, happy, happy.
So I decided it was time to put together a book that would
make even my Grandma Ethel stop and laugh at her hopelessly
pessimistic outlook on life. Too bad she's not still here to read it.
But, then, she never expected to be.

Eric Marcus
January, 2003

P.S. Just a note about the attributions. Where no birth/death
dates are given, that means the quoted individual is alive
(I hope), or I simply could not locate birth/death information.

P.P.S. If you would like to contribute a quote or comment
on this book, contact me through the publisher or through
www.pessimisms.com.

When it came to her view of life, I always thought of my Grandma Ethel as a world-class pessimist. But that was before Leonore Fleischer wrote to me about her mother, Helen, whom Leonore suggested could fill *Pessimisms*—and a few sequels besides—with her thoughts. Leonore wrote: "If you will send me a self-addressed, mother-size box, with a couple of air holes and the proper postage, I will ship you my own personal mother, a woman who, when faced with the classic dilemma 'Is the glass half full or half empty?' can, at one and the same time and without apparent effort, convince you that (a) there is no glass—you're running a temperature and hallucinating; and (b) the glass is chipped and dirty and if you drink from it you'll catch a fatal disease." Sorry Grandma. When it comes to her outlook on life, Leonore's mom sets a standard that you could never have met.

Life is divided into the horrible and the miserable.

— Woody Allen

Birth, *n.* The first and direst of all disasters.
—Ambrose Bierce (1842–1914)

That which does not kill me
only serves to make me suffer.
—Brad Schreiber

A watched pot may never boil.
But an unwatched one always boils over.
—Joan M. Washington

No matter how you look at it,
life is a no-win situation.
—Cynthia Grossman

Our birth is nothing but our death begun.
—Edward Young (1683–1765)

I've learned

to accept

birth

and death

but sometimes

I still worry

about what

lies between.

—© Ashleigh Brilliant

L i f e

Blessed is he who expects nothing,
for he shall never be disappointed.

–Alexander Pope (1688–1744)

Life is easier than you'd think;
all that is necessary is
to accept the impossible,
do without the indispensable,
and bear the intolerable.

–Kathleen Norris (1880–1960)

Every morning signals a new day
during which something can go wrong.

–Bob Uyeda

Why torture yourself
when life will do it for you?

—Laura Walker

Don't worry
about tomorrow;
who knows
what will befall
you today?

—Yiddish folk saying

No good deed
goes unpunished.

—Clare Boothe Luce (1903–1987)

Take courage!
Whatever you decide to do,
it will probably be the wrong thing.

–©Ashleigh Brilliant

**Never face facts;
if you do you'll never get up in the morning.**

–Marlo Thomas

Don't look back.
Something might be gaining on you.

–Satchel Paige (1906–1982)

"What Can You Expect From a Day
That Begins With Getting Up?"

—Wendy R. Ellner

(entry in a *New York* magazine competition
for original country song titles)

I can remember, at the age of five,
being told that childhood was
the happiest period of life
(a blank lie, in those days).
I wept inconsolably,
wished I were dead,
and wondered how I should
endure the boredom
of the years to come.

—Bertrand Russell (1872–1970)

It is a misery to be born, a pain to live,
 a trouble to die.

–St. Bernard of Clairvaux (1090–1153)

There's no limit to how complicated
things can get, on account of one thing
always leading to another.

–E. B. White (1899–1985)

When sorrows come,
 they come not single spies,
But in battalions.

–King, Hamlet, *William Shakespeare (1564–1616)*

He who expects much can expect little.
—*Gabriel García Márquez*

We're all in this alone.
—*Lily Tomlin*

If it's not one thing, it's two.
—*James B. Ledford (1924–1981)*

Ninety percent of life is miserable—if you're lucky.
—*Eric Marcus*

There are
two tragedies
in life.
One is
not to get
your heart's
desire.

The other is to get it.

—George Bernard Shaw
(1856–1950)

Life is snack or famine.

–*Susan Wolbarst*

No matter
what you order
at a restaurant,
what everyone else
orders will look better.

–*Paulina Borsook*

The bread never falls but on its buttered side.

–*English proverb*

An optimist is a guy who has never had much experience.

—*Don Marquis (1878–1937)*

If anything can go wrong, it will.

—*Murphy's Law*
(said to have been invented by
George Nichols in 1949)

Murphy was an optimist.

—*Variously attributed.*

Every day is horrible, so it couldn't get any worse.

—Barbara Giese

I believe in the total depravity
of inanimate things . . .
the elusiveness of soap,
the knottiness of strings,
the transitory nature of buttons,
the inclination of suspenders to twist
and of hooks to forsake their lawful eyes
and cleave only unto the hairs
of their hapless owner's head.

—Katharine Walker (1840–1916)

I'd give up now, but I don't have the time.

—Jane Belenky

Things are going to get a lot worse
before they get worse.

–Lily Tomlin

One day I sat thinking almost in despair;
a hand fell on my shoulder and a voice said
reassuringly: "Cheer up, things could
get worse." So I cheered up and,
sure enough, things got worse.

–James Hagerty (1901–1981)

Life isn't one damn thing after another.
It's the same damn thing again and again.

–Edna St. Vincent Millay (1892–1950)

I always read
the last page
of a book first
so that if I die
before I finish
I'll know how
it turned out.

—Nora Ephron

Less is less.

—*Variously attributed.*

The light at the end of the tunnel is
only a train, and it's not yours anyhow.

—*Author Unknown*

It is wisdom in prosperity,
when all is as thou wouldst have it,
 to fear and suspect the worst.

—*Desiderius Erasmus (1466–1536)*

Life's a rough business,
and nobody will get through it alive.

—*Herbert Frankel*

The situation is hopeless, but not serious.

—Austrian proverb
(as remembered by Rick Stryker's grandmother)

It's always darkest before it goes pitch black.

—Connie Winkler

My mother often told me,
"Marshall, the sooner you learn
that life is 95% misery and only
5% happiness, the better off you'll be."

—Marshall Kirk

Living is a sickness from which
sleep provides relief every sixteen hours.
It's a palliative. The remedy is death.

—Nicolas-Sébastien Chamfort (1741–1794)

Believe nothing and be
on your guard against everything.

—Latin proverb

What is the use of straining after an amiable
view of things, when a cynical view is most
likely to be the true one.

—George Bernard Shaw (1856–1950)

No matter how cynical you get,
 it is impossible to keep up.

—Lily Tomlin

Don't borrow trouble;
it will find you soon enough.

—Betsy Rapoport's Mother and "Gram"

It gets harder the more you know.
Because the more you find out
the uglier everything seems.

—Frank Zappa (1940–1993)

To know all is not to forgive all.
It is to despise everybody.

—Quentin Crisp (1908–1999)

As surely as you try
to impress someone,
you'll do something stupid.

—Tamara Valjean

Life is something that happens to you while you're making other plans.

—Margaret Millar (1915—1994)

For life in general, there is but one decree:
Youth is a blunder, manhood a struggle, old age a regret.

—Benjamin Disraeli (1804–1881)

After a year in therapy, my psychiatrist
said to me, "Maybe life isn't for everyone."

—Larry Brown

When my ship comes in,
with my luck I'll be at the airport.

—John Adey

The examined life is not worth living.

—*Gloria Steinem*
(as told to Suzanne Braun Levine)

Just because you're paranoid doesn't mean they aren't out to get you.

—*Variously attributed*.

One hundred thousand lemmings can't be wrong.

—*Graffiti*

No matter how much you wiggle and dance, the last three drops go down your pants.

—*Author unknown*

Life can be so tragic:
You're here today and here tomorrow.

—©*Ashleigh Brilliant*

Perhaps one day this too
will be pleasant to remember.

–*Virgil (70–19 B.C.)*

This, too, shall pass—just like a kidney stone.

–*Hunter Madsen*

I've always expected the worst,
and it's always worse than I expected.

–*Henry James (1843–1916)*

No issue is so small that it
can't be blown out of proportion.

–*Stuart Hughes*

Life is just a bowl of pits.

—Rodney Dangerfield

She not only
expects the worst,
she makes
the worst of it
when it happens.

—Michael Arlen (1895–1956)

Cheer up, the worst is yet to come.

—Philander Johnson

It's always something.

—Gilda Radner (1947–1989)

We are all dying people.

−Barry Owen

There is no such thing as inner peace.
There is only nervousness and death.

−Fran Lebowitz

Death is not the end.
There remains the litigation over the estate.

−Ambrose Bierce (1842−1914)

We die before we have learned to live.

−Stephen Winsten

The statistics on death are unchanged.

−Author unknown

Expect
the worst.
You won't be
disappointed.

—**Variously Attributed**

Generally speaking, it wasn't in Grandma Ethel's nature to trust people. She viewed everyone who came into her little gift shop in Bay Ridge, Brooklyn, as a potential customer *and* a potential thief—and not necessarily in that order. Often, after browsers had left the store, she'd scan the shelves convinced they'd stolen a china Madonna or a crystal kitty.

Not surprisingly, given the amoral state of humankind, even Grandma's innate pessimism underestimated the potential for thievery. Once, when she was in the stockroom, a customer made off with her solid bronze cash register, a pre-electronic machine as heavy as a bank vault. Despite her girth, flat feet, and advanced age, Grandma took off after the slow-moving criminal and forced him to turn over his prize. The startled thief was lucky—Grandma merely pressed charges. She had threatened to break his neck.

PESSIMISMS

**Most people
would
sooner die
than think;
in fact,
they do so.**

—Bertrand Russell
(1872–1970)

You can always rely on
a society of equals
taking it out on the women.

–Alan Sillitoe

Real equality is going to come
not when a female Einstein is recognized
as quickly as a male Einstein,
but when a female schlemiel
is promoted as quickly
as a male schlemiel.

–Bella Abzug (1920–1998),
(as quoted by Marlo Thomas)

Men are taught to apologize
for their weaknesses,
women for their strengths.

–Lois Wyse

The only time a woman really succeeds in changing a man is when he's a baby.

—Natalie Wood (1938–1981)

Men have a much better time of it than women. For one thing, they marry later; for another thing, they die earlier.

—H. L. Mencken (1880–1956)

Beware of men who cry. It's true that men who cry are sensitive to and in touch with feelings, but the only feelings they tend to be sensitive to and in touch with are their own.

—Nora Ephron

When I

meet a man

I ask myself,

"Is this the man

I want

my children

to spend their

weekends with?"

—Rita Rudner

If you pick up a starving dog
and make him prosperous,
he will not bite you.
This is the principal difference
between a dog and a man.

—Mark Twain (1835–1910)

The more I see of men,
the more I like dogs.

—Madame De Staël (1766–1817)

All I care to know is that a man
is a human being—that is enough for me;
he can't be much worse.

—Mark Twain (1835–1910)

Boys will be boys,
and so will a lot of middle-aged men.

—F. McKinney (Kin) Hubbard (1868–1930)

The belief in a supernatural source of evil
is not necessary; men alone are
quite capable of every wickedness.

—Joseph Conrad (1857–1924)

Men
are like
toilets;
they're either
taken
or
full of it.

—Author Unknown

No one ever went broke
underestimating the taste
of the American public.

–H. L. Mencken (1880–1956)

The public is wonderfully tolerant.
It forgives everything except genius.

–Oscar Wilde (1854–1900)

The difference between genius
and stupidity is that genius has its limits.

–Author unknown

We learn from experience
that men never learn anything from experience.

–George Bernard Shaw (1856–1950)

The 100 percent American is
99 percent an idiot.

–George Bernard Shaw (1856–1950)

People—you can't live with 'em, period.
–*Marshall Kirk*

Human nature is often the greatest
deterrent to making an intelligent decision.
–*Author unknown*

Only two things are infinite,
the universe and human stupidity,
and I'm not sure about the former.
–*Albert Einstein (1879–1955)*

Only the mediocre are always at their best.
–*Jean Giraudoux (1882–1944)*

The best lack all conviction,
while the worst are full of
passionate intensity.

–W.B. Yeats (1865–1939)

No one really listens to anyone else,
and if you try it for a while you'll see why.

–Mignon McLaughlin

Trust everybody, but cut the cards.

–Finley Peter Dunne (1867–1936)

Do not trust to the cheering,
for those very persons
would shout as much if you
and I were going to be hanged.

—Oliver Cromwell (1599–1658)

It is a sin to believe in the evil of others,
but it is seldom a mistake.

—H. L. Mencken (1880–1956)

It's silly to go on pretending that
under the skin we are all brothers.
The truth is more likely that
under the skin we are all
cannibals, assassins, traitors,
liars, hypocrites, poltroons.

—Henry Miller (1891–1980)

The only normal people are the ones
you don't know very well.

—Joe Ancis

Friends

may

come and go,

but

enemies

accumulate.

—Author unknown

Above all else, Grandma Ethel valued her family. Not—need I even mention it—that her family always made her happy. For example, every summer for as long as I can remember and for as long as my mother can remember, Grandma Ethel came back from her summer vacations in the mountains with her half-dozen sisters to proclaim, "I will never, ever, do that again!"

But every year as summer approached, Grandma agreed to spend another vacation with her sisters at the same bungalow colony in the Catskills. For weeks in advance she'd predict in the most pessimistic of tones: "It will be awful! We will fight the whole time!" And year after year, she was right.

It's all relatives.

—Lynda Cury

Family

They fuck you up, your Mum and Dad.
They may not mean to, but they do.
They fill you with all the faults they had
And add some extra, just for you.

—Philip Larkin (1922–1986)

If it's not one thing
it's your mother.

—Variously attributed

As fathers commonly go,
it is seldom a misfortune to be fatherless;
and considering the general run of sons,
as seldom a misfortune to be childless.

—Lord Chesterfield (1694–1773)

**Happiness
is having
a large, loving,
caring,
close-knit family
in another city.**

—George Burns (1896—1996)

The first half of our lives is ruined
by our parents and the second half
by our children.

—Clarence Darrow (1857–1938)

There's nothing wrong with teenagers
that reasoning with them won't aggravate.

—Author unknown

Relations are simply a tedious pack of people
who haven't got the remotest knowledge of
how to live, nor the smallest instinct
about when to die.

—Oscar Wilde (1854–1900),
"The Importance of Being Earnest"

Like lemmings in search of a cliff, we humans are inexorably drawn to the promise of love and marriage. And Grandma Ethel was no exception to this often disappointing quest. (After all, half of all marriages today end in divorce. And more ought to.) But contrary to expectations and experience, Grandma succeeded in love. She found a good man. Unfortunately, he died young, which did nothing to improve Grandma's outlook on life. But then she met another good man, my Grandpa Louie, who had a heart of gold, an effervescent smile, and a strikingly sunny disposition. He adored his Ethel, his step-daughter, and his grandchildren, and was a champion cha-cha dancer besides.

Grandpa Louie was a locksmith, with strong hands and a strong back. And while he never had even a cold, Grandma couldn't help but worry that he would be the first to go. Grandpa Louie always said that it was the worrying that did her in.

PESSIMISMS

**The trouble with
some women
is that they
get all excited
about nothing—
and then
marry him.**

—Cher

Love is a fire.
But whether it is going to
warm your hearth or burn down your house,
you can never tell.

–Joan Crawford (1906–1977)

Every little girl knows about love.
It is only her capacity to suffer
because of it that increases.

–Françoise Sagan

The trouble with loving is that pets don't last
long enough and people last too long.

–Author unknown

Love is ideal. Marriage is real.
The confusion of the two
shall never go unpunished.

–Johann Wolfgang von Goethe (1749–1832)

If you want to read about love and marriage
you've got to buy two separate books.

–Alan King

Love, *n.* A temporary insanity
curable by marriage. . . .

–Ambrose Bierce (1842–1914)

Every man is thoroughly happy
twice in his life: just after he has met
his first love, and just after
he has left his last one.

–H. L. Mencken (1880–1956)

There are two days when a man is a joy:
the day one marries him and the day one buries him.

–Jane Bartlett

The poor wish to be rich,
the rich wish to be happy,
the single wish to be married,
and the married wish to be dead.

–Ann Landers (1918–2002)

It seemed to me that the desire
to get married—which, I regret to say,
I believe is basic and primal in women—
is followed almost immediately
by an equally basic and primal urge—
which is to be single again.

–Nora Ephron

Whether you marry or
whether you don't,
you'll always regret it.

–Paul Brown

Whenever
you want to
marry someone,
go have lunch
with his
ex-wife.

—Shelley Winters

Personally, I think if a woman hasn't met
the right man by the time she's twenty-four,
she may be lucky.

—Deborah Kerr

Keep your eyes wide open before marriage,
and half shut afterwards.

—Variously attributed

Men marry because they are tired,
women because they are curious;
both are disappointed.

—Oscar Wilde (1854–1900),
"A Woman of No Importance"

The woman cries before the wedding;
the man afterward.

—*Polish proverb*

One was never married, and that's his hell;
another is, and that's his plague.

—*Robert Burton (1577–1640)*

A marriage is likely to be called happy
if neither party ever expected to
get much happiness out of it.

—*Bertrand Russell (1872–1970)*

Bride, *n*. A woman with a fine prospect
of happiness behind her.

—Ambrose Bierce (1842–1914)

You enter it living and come out a corpse.

—Sholom Aleichem (1859–1916),

(on the chuppa, the wedding canopy
under which Jewish couples marry)

The only solid and lasting peace
between a man and his wife
is doubtless a separation.

—Lord Chesterfield (1694–1773)

Men and women, women and men.

It will never work.

—Erica Jong

When a girl marries she exchanges the attentions of many men for the inattention of one.

—Helen Rowland (1876—1950)

Marriage, *n*. The state or condition of
a community consisting of a master,
a mistress, and two slaves, making in all, two.

—*Ambrose Bierce (1842–1914)*

The surest way to be alone is to get married.

—*Gloria Steinem*

Matrimony—the high sea for which
no compass has yet been invented.

—*Heinrich Heine (1797–1856)*

Before marriage, a man will lie awake thinking about something you said; after marriage, he'll fall asleep before you finish saying it.

–Helen Rowland (1875–1950)

There is so little difference between husbands
you might as well keep the first.

–Adela Rogers St. Johns (1894–1988)

Trust your husband, adore your husband,
and get as much as you can in your own name.

–Advice to Joan Rivers from her mother

When a man brings his wife flowers
for no reason—there's a reason.

–Molly McGee (1897–1961)

The most difficult year of marriage
is the one you're in.

–Franklin P. Jones

Marriage is a romance in which
the hero dies in the first chapter.

—Author unknown

It begins with a prince kissing an angel.
It ends with a baldheaded man
looking across the table at a fat woman.

—Author unknown

Marriage is a fever in reverse:
It starts with heat and ends with cold.

—German proverb

Marriage is the only war in which you sleep with the enemy.

—Author unknown

I've had my doubts about God and religion since the very beginning of my spiritual education. At the tender age of eight, my parents signed me up for Hebrew school, three afternoons a week. Why, I wondered, were my parents, who had no interest in Judaism and great interest in the teachings of oddly named Indian yogis, consigning me to this fate?

That was just the start of my confusion. In Hebrew school I learned that God was good and that I was among His chosen people. I also learned from Rabbi Weinberger that I was lucky to even be alive, because six million Jews perished in the Holocaust. (This was a good God?) I also learned that God would punish me if I ever set foot in a church or said the name of the "so-called" savior of the Christian people. (Henceforth he was to be known as "J.C.")

But at the same time, I knew that Grandma Ethel, who owned a small gift shop in an Irish-Catholic Brooklyn neighborhood, did a brisk business in religious objects like wooden crosses, china Madonnas, and little portraits of J.C. Not only was she *not* punished for trading in idolatry, she was rewarded financially for selling to the enemy (although there's no telling what happened when she faced her maker).

So it should have come as no surprise to anyone that, by the time I was ready for my Bar Mitzvah, I was pretty certain that God was a fictional character and that, if there was a God, He wasn't a very attentive or good God. But I have to admit that whenever I'm in an airplane, thundering down the runway, I cast all my doubts aside and instinctively say the *Shema*. That's the prayer Jews are supposed to say if they think they're about to die. Just in case there is a God, I figure it couldn't hurt.

The more you complain, the longer God lets you live.

—Lapel button
spotted by Carol Day

When something good happens it's a miracle and you should wonder what God is saving up for you later.

–Marshall Brickman

I'm Jewish. It's Christmas. Things could be better.

–From an ad for Jews for Jesus.

I sometimes think that God in creating man somewhat overestimated his ability.

–Oscar Wilde (1854–1900)

God & Religion

God punishes us by giving us the things we desire.

—Variously attributed.

If God were suddenly condemned
to live the life which he has inflicted
upon men, He would kill himself.

—Alexandre Dumas, fils (1824–1895)

If there's a supreme being, he's crazy.

—Marlene Dietrich (1901–1992)

Fear prophets . . .
and those prepared to die for the truth,
for as a rule they make many others
die with them, often before them,
at times instead of them.

—Umberto Eco

God is love,

but get it

in writing.

—Gypsy Rose Lee (1914–1970)

To Grandma Ethel, the world was a very hostile place that conspired to break our bones, give us colds, and end life early and abruptly. My poor mother, Grandma's only child, was forbidden to do anything risky, like ride a bicycle, swim, or roller skate.

I got off easy. As Grandma's grandchild I only got warnings. For example, every time it rained, Grandma would call and tell me, "Don't go out in the rain without your galoshes or you'll catch pneumonia and die." I may have been a budding pessimist, but I wasn't ready to die, so I followed her instructions religiously. That was three decades ago; I haven't worn galoshes since. Still, whenever I go out in the rain, I feel like I'm tempting the gods, especially because I can hear this little voice with a heavy Polish accent whispering, "People still die from pneumonia. Don't say I didn't warn you."

If it tastes good, it's trying to kill you.

—Roy Qualley

Early to rise and early to bed
Makes a male healthy, wealthy and dead.

—James Thurber (1894–1961)

Doctors are men who prescribe medicines
of which they know little, to cure diseases
of which they know less,
in human beings of whom they know nothing.

—Voltaire (1694–1778)

The only way to keep your health
is to eat what you don't want,
drink what you don't like,
and do what you'd rather not.

—Mark Twain (1835–1910)

Quit worrying about your health. It'll go away.

—Robert Orben

The cardiologist's diet:
If it tastes good, spit it out.

—Paulina Borsook

After my dad's heart attack he stopped smoking,
cut back on drinking, and avoided eating fun food.
When I told him, "Isn't it nice that you'll live longer?"
 he told me in a really disgusted voice,
"You don't really live longer. It just seems like it."

—Nina Puglia

It's no longer a question of staying healthy.
It's a question of finding a sickness you like.

—Jackie Mason

Long meals make short lives.

—Sir John Lubbock, Lord Avebury (1834–1915)

A diet is a plan, generally hopeless, for reducing your weight, which tests your willpower but does little for your waistline.

—Herbert B. Prochnow

Grandma never had anything good to say about getting old. And why should she have? Her arches fell, her eyesight failed, her gums retreated, and everything ached (so she told us repeatedly). I was very young at the time and wondered what all the complaining was about. *Getting old can't be* that *bad,* I thought.

Well, not long ago, as an orthopedic surgeon manipulated my hip, trying to determine what was causing me agonizing pain every time I took a step, I realized that not only was getting old *that* bad, with all its aches, pains, wrinkles, and gray hair, but it starts when you're young and goes on for a long time. If you're lucky.

**One starts
to get young
at the age
of sixty,
and then
it's too late.**

–Pablo Picasso
(1881–1973)

He that is not
handsome at twenty,
nor strong at thirty,
nor rich at forty,
nor wise at fifty,
will never be
handsome, strong,
rich, or wise.

—George Herbert (1593–1633)

At thirty man suspects himself a fool;
Knows it at forty, and reforms his plan;
At fifty chides his infamous delay,
Pushes his prudent purpose to resolve;
In all his magnanimity of thought
Resolves; and re-solves; then dies the same.

—Edward Young (1683–1765)

You should live well into
your senility and beyond.

*—Heard on
"Garrison Keillor's American Radio Company"*

From birth to age eighteen,
a girl needs good parents,
from eighteen to thirty-five
she needs good looks,
from thirty-five to fifty-five
she needs a good personality,
and from fifty-five on she needs cash.

—Sophie Tucker (1884–1966)

Say the woman is forty-four.
Say she is five-seven-and-a-half.
Say her hair is stick color.
Say her eyes are chameleon.
Would you put her in a sack and bury her,
suck her down into the dumb dirt?
Some would,
If not, time will.

—Anne Sexton (1928–1974)

You remember
I used to say
I wanted to die
at thirty—
well, I'm now
twenty-nine and
the prospect
is still welcome.

—F. Scott Fitzgerald (1896—1940)

"Tis strange,
that it is not
in vogue to
commit hara-kari
as the Japanese
do at sixty.
Nature is
so insulting in
her hints
and notices,
does not pull you
by the sleeve,
but pulls out your teeth,
tears off your hair in patches,
steals your eyesight, twists your face
into an ugly mask, in short,
puts all contumelies upon you,
without in the least abating your zeal
to make a good appearance,
and all this is at the same time
that she is moulding the new figures
around you into wonderful beauty
which of course is only making
your plight worse.

—Ralph Waldo Emerson (1803–1882)

Brain weight peaks at
about twenty-five,
and the number of critical cells,
after a period of constancy
from birth to the early twenties,
declines sharply to the nineties.
Each day of our adult lives
more than 100,000 nerve cells die
and nerve cells are never,
of course, replaced.

—Lord Rothschild (1911–1990)

When you are as old as I, young man,
you will know there is only one thing
in the world worth living for, and that is sin.

*—Lady Speranze Wilde (1821–1896),
mother of Oscar Wilde*

Grandma Ethel warned me about politics and politicians. "They're all bums," she told me on more than one occassion, although she always had a warm spot in her heart for F.D.R. and J.F.K. But a decade after Grandma died, full of the optimism of youth, I went to work writing speeches for an elected official in Queens, New York. He was a happy-go-lucky kind of guy. Everyone liked him. He seemed to love his job.

Then one day my boss was implicated as a central figure in a major New York City bribery scandal, and he killed himself. If Grandma had lived to read the headlines, she would have said, "What did I tell you?"

Politics, *n.*
The conduct of
public affairs
for private
advantage.

—Ambrose Bierce
(1842–1914)

Reader, suppose you were
an idiot and suppose you were
a member of Congress.
But I repeat myself.

–Mark Twain (1835–1910)

I don't think that cynicism, disgust,
and apathy is anything other than
a really intelligent response to
the state of American politics.

–Molly Ivins

Those who are too smart
to engage in politics are punished by
being governed by those who are dumber.

–Plato (ca. 428–348 B.C.)

Public office is the last refuge
of the incompetent.

—Boise Penrose (1860–1921)

Democracy is being allowed to vote
for the candidate you dislike least.

—Robert Byrne

Vote for the man who promises least.
He'll be the least disappointing.

—Bernard M. Baruch (1870–1965)

The first mistake in public business
is the going into it.

—Benjamin Franklin (1706–1790)

It doesn't matter who you vote for,
the government always gets in.

–London graffiti

No man will carry out of the presidency
the reputation which carried him into it.

–Thomas Jefferson (1743–1826)

Politics

Every revolution evaporates and leaves behind the slime of a new bureaucracy.

–Franz Kafka (1883–1924)

You are better off not knowing how sausages and laws are made.

–Author unknown

Who thinks the Law has anything to do with Justice? It's what we have because we can't have justice.

–William McIlvanney

You want a friend in Washington? Get a dog.

–Harry S. Truman (1884–1972)

Senate, *n.* A body of elderly gentlemen charged with high duties and misdemeanors.

–Ambrose Bierce (1842–1914)

When I
was a boy
I was told
that anybody
could become
president;
I'm beginning
to believe it.

—Clarence Darrow (1857–1938)

All her life Grandma Ethel looked on the state of the world with a jaundiced eye. She had good reason. Ethel Sand was born at the end of the nineteenth century in Lvov, Austria, grew up in Poland, and in the late 1920s emigrated from what was then the Soviet Union. Funny thing was, before she got on the boat to America, Grandma never ventured far from the city where she was born. It was not Grandma but the borders that kept moving!

Once Grandma got to Brooklyn, except for seasonal pilgrimages to Florida and the Catskills, she stayed put. Grandma was afraid that if she ever left the country, they'd never let her back in. She also had her suspicions about eating at the Greek diner just down the street (where she nonetheless ate every day with Grandpa Louie). Though she was an immigrant, she never trusted foreigners.

123

We have met the enemy and he is us.

—Pogo

The optimist proclaims that we live
in the best of all possible worlds,
and the pessimist fears this is true.

–James Branch Cabell (1879–1958)

Often it does seem a pity that Noah
and his party did not miss the boat.

–Mark Twain (1835–1910)

More than any time
in history mankind
faces a crossroads.
One path leads to despair
and utter hopelessness,
the other to total extinction.
Let us pray that we have the
wisdom to choose correctly.

–Woody Allen

The age of chivalry is gone; that of sophisters, economists, and calculators has succeeded.

–Edmund Burke (1729–1797)

The fundamental cause of trouble in the world today is that the stupid are cocksure while the intelligent are full of doubt.

–Bertrand Russell (1872–1970)

Insanity in individuals is something rare— but in groups, parties, nations, and epochs it is the rule.

–Friedrich Wilhelm Nietzsche (1844–1900)

Correct me if I'm wrong, but hasn't the fine line between sanity and madness gotten finer?

–George Price

PESSIMISMS

This world

is a comedy

to those

who think,

a tragedy

to those

who feel.

—Horace Walpole (1717–1797)

WORK, THE ECONOMY, MONEY, ALCOHOL, ETC.

Grandma Ethel was a very versatile pessimist. No matter what the subject, whether business, money, the weather—you name it—she had an appropriately gloomy sentiment at the ready. "Grandma, how's business?" I would ask. "Could be better," she'd respond. "Grandma, isn't the weather beautiful." I would observe. "Beautiful? You call this beautiful? You could drop dead from sunstroke in such weather," she'd counter. "Grandma, do you think you'll fly to Florida this year?" I'd inquire. "Do you know what happens when a plane hits the ground at hundreds of miles an hour?" she'd reply.

If she'd lived long enough, I would have asked her, "Grandma, do you think this book will be a big hit?" Most likely, she would have answered, "Who would buy such a book?"

In this economy, every silver lining has a dark cloud.

—*Business Week* headline
March 9, 1992

WORK, THE ECONOMY, MONEY, ALCOHOL, ETC.

When things at work are busy and you're harassed and deliveries are late and people are screaming at you and you're getting cancellations, you pray for things to slow down so you can take a breath. Then when things slow down, you wonder if you'll ever do business again. Slow or busy it's never good.

—Richard Marcus

By working faithfully eight hours a day, you may eventually get to be a boss and work twelve hours a day.

—Robert Frost (1874–1963)

WORK, THE ECONOMY, MONEY, ALCOHOL, ETC.

A conference is a gathering of
important people who singly
can do nothing, but together
can decide that nothing can be done.

Fred Allen (1894–1957)

Meetings are indispensable when
you don't want to do anything.

–John Kenneth Galbraith

Men occasionally stumble over the truth,
but most of them pick themselves up
and hurry off as if nothing had happened.

–Sir Winston Churchill (1874–1965)

WORK, THE ECONOMY, MONEY, ALCOHOL, ETC.

Some editors are failed writers,
but so are most writers.

–T. S. Eliot (1888–1965)

The difference between
journalism and literature is that
journalism is unreadable and
literature is not read.

–Oscar Wilde (1854–1900)

Writing is not a profession,
but a vocation of unhappiness.

–Georges Simenon (1903–1985)

Their guess is as good as anybody else's.

–Will Rogers (1879–1935), on economists

There is hardly anything in the world
that some man cannot make a little worse
and sell a little cheaper.

–John Ruskin (1819–1900)

Advertisements contain the only truths
to be relied on in a newspaper.

–Thomas Jefferson (1743–1826)

Save a little money each month
and at the end of the year
you'll be surprised at
how little you have.

–Ernest Haskins

By the time we've made it, we've had it.

–Malcolm Forbes (1919–1990)

I have enough money to last me the rest of my life, unless I buy something.

—Jackie Mason

Miscellaneous

WORK, THE ECONOMY, MONEY, ALCOHOL, ETC.

As scarce as truth is, the supply has always been in excess of demand.

–Josh Billings (1818–1885)

It is by the goodness of God that in our country we have those three unspeakably precious things: freedom of speech, freedom of conscience, and the prudence never to practice either of them.

–Mark Twain (1835–1910)

There are only two ways to telling the complete truth— anonymously and posthumously.

–Thomas Sowell

Alcohol is the anesthesia by which we endure the operation of life.

–George Bernard Shaw (1856–1950)

I'd hate to be a teetotaler.
Imagine getting up in the morning
and knowing that's as good
as you're going to feel all day.

–Dean Martin (1917–1995)

Regarding getting sober:
The good news is you get your life back.
The bad news is you get *your* life back.

–Author unknown

Join the army,
see the world,
meet interesting people,
and kill them.

–Author unknown

The Optimistic Pessimist

If not for Grandma May, who is one of the most optimistic people I know, I would be a true pessimist, just like my Grandma Ethel. But I'm not, so to satisfy the sunny side of my nature, and to acknowledge Grandma May's influence, I've decided to offer a few quotes here that put an optimistic spin on a pessimistic situation or outlook.

You can always succeed at giving up.

—Bob Uyeda

The Optimistic Pessimist

Success is the ability to go from
failure to failure without losing
your enthusiasm.

—Sir Winston Churchill (1874–1965)

One reassuring thing about modern art is that
things can't be as bad as they are painted.

—M. Walthall Jackson

If . . . you can't be a good example,
then you'll just have to be a horrible warning.

—Catherine Aird

Don't take life so seriously . . .
It's not permanent.

—Variously Attributed

The Optimistic Pessimist

I feel much better now that I've given up hope.

—©*Ashleigh Brilliant*

"Constructive depression:
How to make the best of feeling down."

—*Topic included on a videotape for stress management*

One thing about pain:
It proves you're alive.

—©*Ashleigh Brilliant*

The Optimistic Pessimist

Growing old is better than the alternative.

—Variously attributed

The longer I live the less future there is to worry about.

—©Ashleigh Brilliant

I am guardedly optimistic
about the next world,
but remain cognizant of
the downside risks.

—Jeremy Gluck

Razors pain you;
Rivers are damp;
Acids stain you
And drugs cause cramp;
Guns aren't lawful;
Nooses give;
Gas smells awful;
You might as well live.

—Dorothy Parker (1893–1967)

The Ultimate Pessimist

As much as I would like to elevate Grandma Ethel to that peerless pantheon of ultimate pessimists, I can't. Not that Grandma wasn't a first-class pessimist. She was. But, as much as I loved her, I have to admit that she wasn't hard core. We all knew that deep down Grandma Ethel really hoped for the best. But even though Grandma Ethel failed the ultimate pessimist test, there are still many thousands, if not millions, of people scattered across the globe who are convinced that life really is no better than the alternative.

For example, there is my friend Steve Flesch's mother, who when asked what she wanted for her 70th birthday answered: "An easy death." (Fifteen years later, she was indeed granted her wish.)

The Ultimate Pessimist

And then there is Tamar Kipper's grandmother, a perennially pessimistic soul, who, like my Grandma May, started life in Warsaw, Poland. From an early age, Tamar did her best to bring a little sunlight into her grandmother's day. Once, while visiting her grandmother in Israel, eighteen-year-old Tamar pointed out some roadside flowers in glorious bloom. "Grandma," she said, "aren't the flowers beautiful?" Grandma's response: "Yes, but like people, they die, too."

If you recognize yourself in these last few pages, count yourself among that special class of people who, like Steve Flesch's mother and Tamar Kipper's grandmother, are ultimate pessimists.

A pessimist is one who has been intimately acquainted with an optimist.

—Elbert Hubbard
(1856–1915)

The Ultimate Pessimist

Do you know what a pessimist is?
A man who thinks everybody
as nasty as himself, and hates them for it.

—George Bernard Shaw (1856–1950)

A pessimist is one who feels bad when he feels good
for fear he'll feel worse when he feels better.

—Author unknown

When two pessimists meet
they shake heads instead of hands.

—Hunter Madsen

When the cat's away,
chances are he's been run over.

—Michael Sanders

A pessimist is one who,
when he has the choice of two evils,
chooses both.

—Author unknown

An optimist sees an opportunity in every calamity;
a pessimist sees a calamity in every opportunity.

—Author unknown

How happy are
the pessimists!
What joy is theirs
when they have
proved there is
no joy.

*—Marie von Ebner-
Eschenbach
(1830–1916)*

The Ultimate Pessimist

One has to have the courage
of one's pessimism.

–Ian McEwan

My pessimism goes to the point of
suspecting the sincerity of pessimists.

–Jean Rostand (1894–1977)

Pessimism in our time is infinitely
more respectable than optimism:
The man who foresees peace,
prosperity, and a decline in
juvenile delinquency is a negligent
and vacuous fellow.
The man who foresees catastrophe
has a gift of insight which insures
that he will become a
radio commentator, an editor of *Time*,
or go to Congress.

–John Kenneth Galbraith

PESSIMISMS

I was going to
buy a copy of
*The Power of
Positive Thinking,*
and then
I thought:
What the
hell good
would that do?

—Ronnie Shakes

Acknowledgments

In a world filled with hopeless optimists, I was heartened to discover more than a handful of kindred spirits who can't help but see the glass as half empty, especially my friend Barbara Moulton, whose ideas and encouragement led to the publication of *Expect the Worst (You Won't Be Disappointed)*, the 1992 book on which this book is based.

To those who contributed their original bleak thoughts, I am forever grateful (with "forever," you can never be too sure). And many thanks to those of you who brought appropriately pessimistic quotes to my attention, particularly Robert Abramson, Simeon Baum, Lila Bellar, Frank Browning, Tina Collen, Leonore Fleischer, David Frankel, Robert Getlan, Joan Lexau, Ann Northrop, Barry Owen, Donald Poynter, Joel Roselin, Toni Sciarra, the late Randy Shilts, Christian Skeem, Georgette Weir, and John Wolf.

I am also compelled to thank the following people for their help in giving this book a new life as *Pessimisms*. These include: Barney Karpfinger, Michael Murphy (and the staff at CDS), Joy Harris (and the staff at The Joy Harris Literary Agency, especially Alexia Paul), James Wade, Andrew Collen at Happy Trails Annimation,

Acknowledgments

Jen Richards and Rachel Tarlow Gul at Over the River Public Relations, and my cousin, Elliot Joel Stern, a kindred spirit and talented designer who never said, "Who would buy such a book?"

Grateful acknowledgment is made for permission to reprint from the following:

Excerpt from "This be the Verse" from *Collected Poems* by Philip Larkin. © 1988, 1989 by the Estate of Philip Larkin. Reprinted by permission of Farrar, Straus and Giroux, LLC.

"Resume," from *Dorothy Parker: Complete Poems* by Dorothy Parker, copyright © 1999 by The National Association for the Advancement of Colored People. Used by permission of Penguin, a division of Penguin Group (USA).

"Hurry Up Please It's Time," reprinted by permission of Sterling Lord Literistic, Inc. Copyright Anne Sexton.